The Heart of a Young Prophet

Written by: Misha Wesley

Copyright © 2017 by Misha Wesley.

All rights reserved
Rejoice Essential Publishing
P.O. BOX 85
Bennettsville, SC 29512
www.republishing.org

All rights reserved. No part of this book may be used or reproduced by any means, graphic, electronic, or mechanical, including photocopying, recording, taping or by any information storage retrieval system without the written permission of the publisher except in the case of brief quotations embodied in critical articles and reviews.

Unless otherwise indicated, Scripture is taken from the King James Version.

Scriptures taken from the Holy Bible, New International Version®, NIV®. Copyright © 1973, 1978, 1984, 2011 by Biblica, Inc.™ Used by permission of Zondervan. All rights reserved worldwide. www.zondervan.com™

Scriptures taken from The Holy Bible, New Living Translation, copyright ©1996, 2004, 2007. Used by permission of Tyndale House Publishers, Inc., Carol Stream, Illinois 60188.

Visit the author's website at www.Apostolicfirestarter.com

While the author has made every effort to provide accurate internet addresses at the time of publication, neither the publisher nor the author assumes any responsibility for errors or for changes that occur after publication.

Heart Of A Young Prophet/Misha Wesley

ISBN-10:1-946756-04-0
ISBN-13:978-1-946756-04-6

Library of Congress Control Number: 2017942251

ACKNOWLEDGEMENTS

Jesus died for our sins and by his stripes we are healed! I have to give thanks to the man I love so dearly, my husband of 10 years, he pushed and supported my dream of becoming a published author. Though we are not perfect, God is perfecting our love and marriage each and every day!

Big thanks to Clay Nash for covering me, supporting me, providing the atmosphere conducive to groom the prophetic gift in me, praying in agreement with me for the production of this book and of who I am sent to be; My best friend and sister Alexis Gwinn Miller, which encouraged me, and drew out the wisdom of the Word to groom me into the office of the Prophet. I love you sis! Amen!

Table Of Contents

ACKNOWLEDGEMENTS...iii
INTRODUCTION..1
PRAYER FOR A PURE HEART....................................7
SOUL...9
BROKENHEARTED..16
POEM FOR PROPHETS..19
DELIVERANCE...22
HOLINESS AND RIGHTEOUSNESS..........................31
HEART..37
THE HEART OF SPIRITUAL WARFARE...................43
THE CALLING DREAM...49
BREAKING THROUGH HARD GROUND 51
YOUR MINISTRY BEGINS RIGHT WHERE YOU ARE........60
SPIRIT..65
THE RIVER OF THE PROPHETIC..............................67
THE PUSH AND RELEASE..77
THE SET UP FOR ALL..81

CHAPTER ONE

Introduction

What is a Prophet and how can we identify one? Good question, and I will further explain. The prophet's ministry is designed by God to help protect the church from the devices, attacks, and plans of hell. God speaks through his Prophets and through them he sends his plans, messages, and wisdom. Some leaders and people in the church don't believe in the prophet's ministry because of misrepresentation or abuse, and I get that. However, we can tell by the fruit, which means the character, of a true Prophet. 1 John 4:1: We should try the spirit by the spirit, and every true prophet must possess the fruit of the spirit which is love, joy, peace, forbearance, kindness, gentleness, and most importantly self-control. Galatians 5:22: The true call of a prophet first starts with God choosing from the womb, whom he appoints as his Prophets. Then, the Lord leads the Prophet on a journey of self-cleansing and healing of heart. The condition of the heart is God's biggest concern, which leads us to walk in righteousness or in wickedness. If our heart is after Christ, then out of our mouths will then pour the words of Christ and our lives will reflect the ways of our father in heaven, and His ways are righteous and true. The Prophet's ministry brings with it the power to preserve.

In Hosea 12:13: And by a prophet the LORD brought Israel out of Egypt, and by a prophet was he preserved. The prophet's ministry is to guard, preserve, protect, and keep, which there is a Shamar aspect of a prophet's ministry of guarding; people, cities, regions and territories. Prophets are strong builders and restorers. You simply cannot stick prophets in the corner and say pray, only because prophets do much more in the body of Christ and are called to teach, train and equip, the body of Christ (Ephesians 4:11).

We know the blueprints and patterns from heaven for building. The office of the prophet is more than just prophesying or singing anointed songs, having visions and dreams. Prophets water and bring refreshing, prophets bring correction; prophets have a strong releasing anointing, they help release people into their destiny. In 1 Samuel you notice the prophet Samuel was used by God to anoint David; 1 Samuel 16:13: and when Samuel anointed Saul; 1 Samuel 10:1. Prophets have a strong breakthrough anointing and a strong deliverance anointing. As Jeremiah 1:10, prophets are designed to root out spirits of wickedness and pull down strongholds built by the enemy, destroy walls and barriers, throw down, build and plant. Prophets break down hard walls and help others enter into new realms of the spirit. When Prophets prophesy, they speak God's word like fire and as a hammer! This hammer breaks the rock into pieces Jeremiah 23:29.

The fire spoken of in Jeremiah 23:29 is a purifying type of fire; this fire is figurative for a corrective word that brings deliverance, which is healing. The governmental authority, meaning they declare the promises of God into the person's life, setting people into God's order where the foundation can be laid in the person's life as they speak. The person hears the word you're delivering because it's said with more authority that God has spiritually imparted from heaven. This is what makes this ministry and office of the prophet more of a setting and releasing, it is of God's governmental authority.

Prophets do tend to have more visions, dreams, see into the spirit realm, they operate in words of wisdom, words of knowledge, and strong discerning of spirits. Many are different but should bear the same fruit of the spirit and should ALL recognize Jesus as Lord and Savior! I want to just break the confusion right now and distinguish between prophets and Psychics. Psychics are demonic and operate through familiar spirits, and receive much of their information from demons. In the book of Acts 16:16 it speaks of Paul and Silas interacting with a slave girl in which could predict the future and foretell future events. Because this girl operated through a familiar spirit or divination, it angered Paul and he then proceeded to cast the demon out of the girl. The Bible actually speaks of God turning his face against those who operate in witchcraft. Psychics are a perverted form of a prophet because ALL true prophets get all their information from God!

As a leader, I believe in transparency and I strongly urge you to as well. Transparency is the most imperative aspect of a successful ministry. If you can't be transparent in whom you are or the darkness you were bound in, what makes you think you can bring deliverance to someone else? What makes you think that if you're not honest with yourself, that someone else will be honest with you? How can you expect to evangelize and save souls if you have not come out of agreement with your demons? I ask you this because I am about to take you inside of my heart, and the heart God created in me. The call God has on my life is one in which I must be truthful with myself and you, my readers. So many pastors and leaders in the church are afraid of saying or speaking about the darkness in which they came and some refuse to come out of agreement with sinful lifestyles, but not me.

We all have been saved when Jesus died on the cross but we need to be delivered from the demonic oppression, delivered from the trauma of your childhood, young adulthood, and delivered so that you can walk worthy of your calling. I am not just one with another prophetic story, or one that has had a glorious encounter with God, but a real life transformational story. "A road to Damascus" Journey in Acts 9, when the Apostle Paul seen Christ and immediately following that experience, he was never the same! I too was immediately transformed from Misbah to Misha! Finally taking up with me my true identity in Christ. I'm not going to sugar coat my path but expose the righteous and holy path it takes to please God! I learned a very important nugget of wisdom from Prophet Kevin Leal that created in my heart conviction for truth in transparency: "You never know if your dirt may save someone else!"

As you read this book, you will have an inside look at The Heart of a Young Prophet. the making, the shaking, the beating, and the pressings of my life. I'll take you on an in-depth journey into that transitional dimension into the office of the prophet. I want to lead you towards The environment it takes to groom the prophetic gift and to stir up the gift of God that is inside you. The heart I carried was not my own, but the heart of God. God has raised me up and made me in the wilderness, which means a dry place that caused a stretching of my capacity; mentally, emotionally, and physically. However, it was in those dry places, God brought water, and bread for me to eat, as I leaned unto him with my whole heart. This is a true story of the heart of God in which many prophets carry.

Many of you reading this book have dreams, hopes and gifts. Each of you are destined with God's plans, and his purpose's. It's downloaded deeply within the wells of your souls. His plans+ His purpose=your DESTINY! However, to discover your destiny, you must to allow Jesus Christ into your hearts and serve him with gladness. The understanding I want you to have is that the Lord takes pleasure in the prosperity of his servant; Psalms 35:27. We are the Lord's servants! A servant means to be a devoted and helpful follower or supporter; performing duties for others. In order to perform duties for others or to be a helpful follower of Christ, it starts with having the heart of a servant. Having a heart to serve is having the heart of God. After all, that is what the kingdom of God is. It's not about YOU, or even giving yourself a name, but it's for the name of the father and the son. God is concerned with the condition of our hearts. Before we go any further we must pray:

CHAPTER TWO

Prayer For A Pure Heart

Purifying the heart with prayer

PRAYER TO RECEIVE A PURE HEART

Heavenly father forgive me of my sins and forgive us of our transgressions

Create in me a pure heart, O God, and renew a steadfast spirit within me, Psalms 51:10

Restore to me the Joy of your salvation and grant me a willing spirit, to sustain me. Psalms 51:12

Search me oh God, and know my heart, try me and know my thoughts,

and see if there be any wicked way in me, and lead me in the way of everlasting Psalms 139:23-24

Lord create in me a pure heart.

Father in the name of Jesus, I command all spiritual cataracts to fall!

I command all blinders to be lifted off my eyes, in the name of Jesus

Give me an ear to hear what the spirit of the lord says Rev 2:29

I am your servant o lord prosper me! Lord you take pleasure in my prosperity Psalms 35:27

I receive the gift of revelation through the prophetic anointing! I receive a fresh anointing!

In Jesus' name amen!

CHAPTER THREE

My existence of where I came; emotions and the start of life

The Lord called me before my birth;

from within the womb he called me by name.

He made my words of judgment as sharp as a sword.

He has hidden me in the shadow of his hand.

I am like a sharp arrow in his quiver.

Isaiah 49:1-2

When the Lord called me, chose me and sent me, I was in my mother's womb. Born into the world with two names, similar to the Apostle Paul, whose former name was Saul. Throughout my entire life, everyone has called me Misbah and I actually begun to believe this was my name. However, at the time of my birthing, the nurses placed the name on my birth certificate as "Misha", which means "God like". My mother tried to change this, however, she was unsuccessful. Misbah is an Arabic name meaning light, bright light and is unisex for boys and for girls. For the duration of my childhood, I was raised Muslim.

I was raised with my Mother and father, 4 sisters and little brother that was 3 years younger than me. I spent the majority of my childhood and young adult years being called Misbah. As a child, I watched as my father and my uncles as they made salot. Women were never able to partake in the calling of the athon. Sadly, women in this culture are demeaned and frowned upon. Not even is a woman allowed to be around other males within the same masque or calling of prayer. Let me be perfectly clear, women can go to mosques. However, it is separated by gender; men with men and women with women. When a woman is on her menstrual cycle, it's deemed an abomination or just plain "unclean" to be around the others when praying, so she is told to seclude herself to pray or make other religious offering to their God. The mosque in Muslim culture is like the meeting and gathering place where mainly Muslim men come together.

I didn't know anything as a child about this Allah, I just knew we had to make salot 6 times a day, and perform a religious ritual called; wudhu before we prayed. Wudhu is a ritual that Muslims perform before they pray. This ritual is supposed to make them clean before their God, they're also to wear good clothing. As I got older I learned so much as I watched so much. I was never able to speak as my father raped and abused my sisters. He hid the brutal abuse so very well from his family and friends and as a result, many of my sisters were unable to speak out and tell someone what was happening. I remember one day as he brutally attacked my sister, he was stepping on her stomach repeatedly over and over again. Everyone stood around watching, even my mother, but something rose up inside of me and with a boisterous tone, as a 6 year old, I said, 'Stop it now!" and immediately, he stopped.

This was very shocking to see him drop what he was doing and leave. They all stared at me, confounded at my authority and the result of what I said to my father. Fortunately, my father never touched me or abused me. My sisters were bewildered, and my mother was too. Many of them thought he wanted to spare me, and many of them thought that he spoiled me for some odd reason. Nevertheless, they resented me for this and secretly picked on me and often tormented me. This is what set me apart as he abused the rest. I remember my sisters was sent out on an errand to the grocery store. They forgot something at the store that our father told us to get. Not wanting to go back to the store because we were tired of walking nearly 7 or 10 miles and it was extremely hot outside, I told them I would say it was my fault and take the blame. I knew that if they would say it was their fault, they would be tortured, maybe killed. As we went home, my father became angry and began to yell at them. He didn't bother even to ask what happened, he just began to prepare to attack them.

They weren't saying anything, they were just shrieking in terror and crying. I stood out from them and said, "it was my fault, dad, I lost it! They didn't do anything!" he looked at them with rage and immediately stopped what he was doing and looked at me menacingly. He gave me a deep stare in my eyes, but I stared back into his not breaking his gaze. He dropped his belt and torture plans and left the room. As he walked out, he said "y'all are lucky, she saved your life!" I hugged my sisters and they thanked me. After that, I remember my father bringing me into another room to threaten my life, telling me never to stand up for them again. And if I did, I would get the same brutal treatment as them. However, I looked him right in the eyes as I did before and he released me and told me to get out of his face. One day as the entire family slept, I remember sharing a room with my sisters, but my bed was near the window.

I looked up out the window and gazed intently at the moon. I remember so clearly the feeling of that night as I began to cry deeply and sob quietly without waking anyone. I became good at being a silent crier. But on this night when I prayed, I was so hurt and wanted my dad to stop hurting my sisters so I cried out to God. I asked God to stop him from hurting them, please! I begged God! Later that week, there was a loud BANG at the front door. When my mother went to the door, there was a man on the other side that said, "OPEN UP, IT'S THE POLICE!"

instead of opening the door, my mother ran to my father who was laying down in the bedroom surrounded by my sisters, ordering them to massage him and rub his feet. "THE POLICE ARE AT THE DOOR!" she shrieked. He got up nervously and stricken with fear. He tried to think quickly what to do and where to run and hide. Without any further waiting, the swat team busted through the door! They came straight for my dad, as if the cops had mapped out my house and hogged tied my father. They then hurled him into the patrol car. I remember my father yelling from the police car window for us to call his long time mistress to help bail him out of jail. However, that never happened!

Later my mother moved us back to New York far away from Virginia where my father was arrested. I didn't see my father again for several years. However, he was finally released from prison and came to get me and my brother, then later sent for my 3rd eldest sister to move from New York to Virginia.

As I later learned, that the hand of God was upon my life. From a child, my demonized father was not able to hurt me, rape me or even lay a finger on my head. How could it have been that I was so special? I was nothing, right? I later learned I would be a rescuer of all God's people, trapped and enslaved in religion and tradition.

In elementary school, I began to stand up for the ones who were being bullied in school. The ones who didn't have a voice, I stood up for them and protected them. The bullies never bullied me, in fact they left me alone. Even though I dressed in hand-me-downs, with tattered clothes, I was never bullied. I was extremely smart, and kept my head buried in a book all the time. I wrote a lot and always studied. I was always the odd ball because of this, and I never fit in. At the age of 10, my father converted to Christianity, and we went to church. However, going to a building to hear a good sermon never changed the monster within him, or who he was. He often attacked my third older sister. So every night, I got on bended knees, bowed my head and I prayed to God, not Allah, so that he wouldn't hurt her and it worked! There was much peace after I prayed, so I kept doing it! No one taught me to pray, nor did I watch anyone pray in this manner. I just had a feeling to do it, so I did! You may think this was strange and it doesn't make sense, but to me, at the time, it made perfect sense.

My father died when I was 12 years old. Then my mother came down to Virginia from New York. When they all came down for the funeral, she told me I was coming to live with her in NY and continue school. As I grew older, my mother was in such a great depression from the death of my father. She kept a poor state of mind and refused to find good work. She left my sisters to care and look after me. She burdened them with false responsibility to care for me and my brother. They all tried as best as they could to help me and my little brother. I was often very lonely in New York as my sisters went about their lives. To ward off the rejection I felt, I began writing, more and more every day. I made friends eventually, however, it wasn't enough. I needed my mother, but she was never there to comfort me and love me. I cried many nights in the other room but she ignored me.

Not because she was angry, but because she was unaware of how to comfort herself. She was depressed and unable to give anything emotionally to anyone. Over time I grew angry with her, and rebelled as a result. I did things to try and grab her attention, like stay out late with boys, or just with friends. I didn't even want to go back home sometimes because I felt no love or acceptance from her, so I rejected myself. After my sisters grew up and moved out the house, it was only my little brother and I. My mother left me to care for him, and that same false responsibility fell upon my shoulders. My heart was shattered and I became broken, I saw things a young child should never be exposed too. I was left alone to fend for myself in the darkness of this world. Yet, I wasn't alone and God still loved me, still favored me.

God kept me from the dangerous hands of pimps that lurked around the corner to take a young girl into their sex trafficking schemes and those who sought to have my life! The biggest thing about this whole story is that "I DIDN'T KNOW!" most of the legal rights or open doors we give to the enemy come as a result of a lack of knowledge. In Hosea 4:6, NIV, it says, "My people are destroyed from a lack of knowledge". However, in another translation of the same verse, it replaces "lack of knowledge" with they "don't know me". So many people are being destroyed from simply not knowing Christ and to properly know Christ only comes through a deep intimacy and relationship. There was a spiritual deficiency in my childhood home which resulted in my later arrested development. The basis of solid relationship with Christ is crucial for the very survival in this treacherous world.

CHAPTER FOUR

Brokenhearted

Searching for closeness in my marriage

The Lord is close to the brokenhearted and saves those who are crushed in spirit Psalms 34:18

    The Lord used a specific covenant in my life to draw me nearer and deeper unto him. He used the most brutal, and traumatic experience of my life to mold me and shape the heart within me. He used my marriage as a template for him to build the prophetic and intercession ministry, he used this as a means to dissect my heart, plant within my soul his seeds of purification and also to extract the wisdom from this hard place which to receive the revelation of the high honor he places upon this covenant.

During this specific season of my life, I stayed in Norfolk, Virginia with my sister, too afraid to live alone. I was separated from my husband, and I was in a state of confusion, hurt and pain. There was nothing at this time I was able to even give myself, let alone anyone else. Like my mother, I was depressed, falling into the same cycle of despair. My heart was torn because my marriage was broken, shattered into a hundred pieces. Like a foolish woman, I tore down my own house with my bare hands. I was blind to the real enemy of this battle and soon I would face that enemy on the front lines, but first, God had to take me and restore me, he had to deliver me, heal me, and close the many doors that I myself opened and that were opened as a result of trauma from my childhood. I remember coming to Christ in prayer begging for him to restore my marriage, restore my family and remove all the brokenness.

Every night I would go into the room where no one was looking and get on my knees and cry out to the Lord. I literally sat on my knees for hours crying and pouring my heart out to him. In that moment, the Lord heard my cries and began to speak to me. I allowed him to come into me and begin to restore me Revelation 3:20. I cried out to the lord with a sorrow-filled cry. My soul was pleading for redemption and freedom as it was shackled and filled with sin. My heart rejoiced with happiness because his face was rising upon me.

Psalms 42:1-11 was my plea to him. I stripped myself and he stripped my soul from every burden. I took up my cross and left my own life behind. My soul thirsted for God, for the living God (Psalms 42:2). My tears had been my meat day and night (Psalms

42:3). When I remember these things, I pour out my soul in me (Psalms 42:4). Yet the Lord commanded his loving kindness in the daytime and in the night his song is with me, and this my prayer unto the God of my life (Psalms 42:8). Where there is ruin, there is hope for a treasure. I was the ruin, but because of Christ I had hope and through his life, he made me a treasure.

What came after this intense season of deep intercession and personal submission, was restoration and a wilderness season.

CHAPTER FIVE

Poem For Prophets

The heart of the prophet is deep and with much tender care

We dream dreams and have visions

We fight tradition and religion

We pluck up and throw down

We overthrow church systems and programs

We build and plant

Prophets love the glory and the presence of god

We cry out to god with a glory chant

The prophet sees what no one else can't

the prophet stands out with ease

We're the insider that thinks like an outsider

Prophets are grieved by staleness and complacency

Prophets hate double mindedness and confusion

And A lukewarm church clouded with delusion

Prophets are not impressed with big buildings and fancy pews

Prophets love genuine repentance and when people are true

Prophets never compromise their beliefs to agree with the world

We walk in the spirit and rebuke lusts of the flesh

Prophets are intercessors and prayer warriors

We push and inspire

We encourage others to bring out their fire

Prophets are fanatical over the top and radical

Prophets are not naysayers and people pleasers!

God always takes care of his prophets

Providing love and much protection

Our cups overflow with favor and progression

We're conquerors and warriors

We're victors and never victims

Arise prophets and come out of your caves your hiding ends

here!

The deliverance for America is near!

CHAPTER SIX

Deliverance

Casting out the enemy from your life

He sent his word and healed them, and delivered them from their destruction Psalms 107:20

It's important to receive deliverance before we move into the higher realms of the spirit. Every level of spiritual warfare presents its own set of challenges and opposition. Do not be deceived and wise in your own eyes, to think the devil will not deceive you, perverting our gifts and talents. The scripture presents a solid biblical foundation on deliverance, in which I will further break down. The New Living Translation actually replaced the last part of the scripture in the King James Version and it says that, "Jesus snatched them from the door of death". Indeed, deliverance for me was definitely Jesus snatching me. However, he also cleansed me, healed me and rescued me from my own destruction.

Deliverance is not something that is often preached about, talked about or discussed. Mainly because the western church has turned sermons into self-improvement messages on how to be a better "you". Whatever that means. How can you be a better you without the help of Christ? How can we overcome addictions? How can we overcome rejection, or overcome the spirit of rebellion? How can we be restored the years the swarming locusts, the cankerworm, the palmer worm and caterpillar ate up our harvest? But it is only through Christ. For it is the love of Christ that surpasses all understanding; Ephesians 3:19. I know it's hard to love someone who does not love you, or love someone that hates you and accuses you. But without Christ, we will not be successful at loving deeply or at forgiving! Not by might nor by power, but by my spirit, says the Lord of Hosts; Zechariah 4:6. Nothing is done in our own strength, but it all is done by the power of the spirit of God!

Now our father is mighty and worthy to be praised for bringing deliverance to my life when I never even knew it existed! One year after I moved to Memphis, TN, I experienced Jesus snatching me from the door of death and bringing me deliverance. I was at work on my lunch break, sitting in the parking lot of my workplace building. I was parked off to the side listening to a well-known prophetess explaining her dream of the last days on Periscope. As I sat and listened, I could feel my throat become dry and I felt a warm sensation all over my body as she spoke in tongues. The tongues she spoke were like fire, touching the inner most parts of my soul. As I listened, I heard very clearly in her tongues "cleanse your soul before it's consumed with fire!" I began to feel a conviction in my heart, I wanted to change and be different. At that moment, I hated my sin.

I hated the underworld I have been a part of and I wanted out right then at that very moment. I heard her say, "If you want to be free and accept Christ, say Jesus, I surrender!" When I said that I immediately began to cry. Rivers of tears flowed from my eyes. I felt so much conviction, warmth and a deep love for Christ, that I never felt. She told us to say it again, and again, and again, I did. Then she said, "I want you to say, I submit my life to you Christ!" When I said this, almost immediately, my body fell limp in my front driver seat. I lost all control of my muscles, fingers and eyes. I pretty much blacked out. As I was sprawled out in my front seat, having no ability to control my body whatsoever, I felt my body convulsing. My chest moving up and down. I could feel what was happening because I was still conscious of my surroundings and I could still hear and feel, but I just couldn't see. I felt sedated almost. When I finally gained control of my body, I opened my eyes to look around. No one was in the parking lot of my job and no one was able to see inside as I had very dark tinted windows. As I got up to walk back inside my workplace, I noticed the time and I had 7 minutes to spare. I gathered myself and got out and as I walked I felt so very light, like I just lost 8 or 10Ibs.

After this shocking ordeal, I kept having dreams of myself laying hands on so many people. I repetitively had dreams where I laid my hands on babies, adults of old and young alike; they seemed to be tormented with demons and as I laid my hands on them, and I spoke in tongues, and they became healed. I kept having dreams hearing the audible voice of the Lord. His voice was quiet, still, no tone, just extremely calm and I can still hear as if it was yesterday, him telling me "you are my intercessor."

A few days later as I sat in church, I remember seeing a preview of Rebecca Greenwood's class; Regional Transformation Warfare School. As the preview went off, I heard the leader say, "If this is you, and you love prayer, or maybe you want to grow in this area of intercessory than this class is for you!" I asked the Lord immediately what to do, and he brought me back to what he told me in the dream. Within my spirit I felt an instant confirmation and agreement.

The first day of class, they asked us to say something about ourselves and when I did, I recalled the deliverance dreams I was having, and explained that I know I have been called and sent to this level of warfare because of the dreams I have been experiencing, not only the dreams, but deliverance! Through this class, it was for me to meet the Apostle that founded the ministry Spiritual Cleansing; getting to the root. It was through this class that I was connected divinely to be cleansed and made whole, through deliverance, for me to walk in my calling. Prophets and Prophetic people need deliverance; really ALL PEOPLE do. Before we can hear the voice of God, before we flow prophetically and prophesy, before we see into the seer realm, we need to be cleansed thoroughly from our sins and walk in righteousness and holiness. The enemy will take advantage of every weakness we have if we are not cleansed from the inside out. First wash the inside of the cup and the dish, and then the outside will become clean, too; Matthew 23:26. Jesus proclaimed to the Pharisees, they are so careful to clean the outside of the cup and the dish, but inside, they were full of greed and wickedness; Luke 11:39.

On 3/25, shortly after my deliverance, I wrote this Revelation the Father provided to me while in deep prayer and meditation. The Lord spoke to me today. As I cried out and read Psalms 84:1-12, which is a prayer of longing for the sanctuary and desperately desiring to be in the Lord's presence. As I read, my heart opened and cried along. When I finished reading, I was asking the Lord that I desired to feel his heartbeat, hear his voice, and be his mouthpiece. Then I picked up my Bible and opened it, my eyes fell on 3 John 1-14. My heart and spirit cried out in unison and in thanksgiving. The Lord is pleased with my obedience, and that there's no greater joy than to hear that my children walk in truth; 3 John 1:4. I held the Holy Bible to my chest and waited with open ears and with all my heart.

Then he spoke: I am causing a great awakening to take place within you, I will pour out my spirit upon you... In the intimate session he said more, but what is key here is the way My Father spoke. He spoke prophetically, prophesying to me, his voice deep and still, calm and loving; tender even. I've never heard him like this before! A day ago, I was delivered and before then, he spoke but in bits and pieces. However, this time, it was clear! There was a demonic interference that occurred in my bloodline and past that kept me from hearing clearly the voice of God! Deliverance gave me a clean ear to HEAR!

As I stated, our bloodline can carry demonic influence that can trap us and keep us bound, keeping us from enjoying the fruits of our labor. In the book of Genesis it describes the punishment God placed upon Cain for the murder of his brother. A punishment which cursed him and his descendants. The LORD said, "What have you done? Listen! Your brother's blood cries out to me from the ground. Now you are under a curse and driven from the ground, which opened its mouth to receive your brother's blood from your hand. When you work the ground, it will no longer yield its crops for you. You will be a restless wanderer on the earth (Genesis 4:10-14). The Vagabond[1] spirit is a generational curse which causes one to wander endlessly, from job to job, houses to house, church to church, relationship to relationship. This spirit is not a wicked mindset, but will affect the descendants as a result of sin. Curses are very real, and so is healing and deliverance from these wicked spirits plaguing the blood-line.

We can try with all our might to change and be better; however, without deliverance and the renewed mind of Christ, demons will lay dormant waiting for a legal right to surface. Demons are legalist and operate by legal authority. They need a right, a door to operate, a connection to the host. Sometimes we inflict pain on ourselves and it may not be a result of anything generational. However, our bloodline carries much of this legal authority a demon needs to operate in a person's life. Past sin from our mothers, fathers, grandfathers, great-grands and so on. For example, a child whose father or grandfather, that participated in freemasonry in the 1st, 2nd, 3rd degree or even up to the 33rd degree would need deliverance.

As we look at the book of Psalms, we see that Psalms consists of 150 poems of Israel written at different times calling out to the Lord. Many of the Psalms rejoice in God's deliverance from trouble (Psalms 91:14-15), Deliverance from a strong enemy (Psalms 18:17-20;48), delivering us from destruction and sometimes our own destruction in which we caused pain, placing us into being victimized and condemnation from the enemy (Psalms 107:19-20). The Bible teaches that deliverance means to be restored, saved or rescued from something; to be brought back from something, and that something is sin. I was removed from the darkness and placed into the light of Christ as he snatched me up! Ephesians 5:8 says that for once you were full of darkness, but now you have light from the lord. So live as people of the light!

This scripture allows us to understand that we ALL were once in darkness; darkness meaning a place of no truth, no knowledge, no understanding. For if we have darkness in us how can we see? for our steps are hidden and we cannot see where we go. But if we have light, our steps are illuminated and revealed to us by our father; He allows us to see what is in front of us! Deliverance is part of redemption, which was accomplished by Jesus on the cross (Colossians 1:13-14). The Greek word for saved or salvation means deliverance, which is pronounced "Sozo".[2] This means to deliver, protect, heal, preserve, save, do well, be whole, rescue, safety, healthy. The Greek is still used for translation because the very first translation of the Hebrew Bible was into Greek, and there are still words that need to be broken down further from Greek to English for our further understanding.

The books of Matthew, Luke, and John records the Gospel of Christ and his ministry, And you know that God anointed Jesus of Nazareth with the Holy Spirit and with power. Then Jesus went around doing good and healing all who were oppressed by the devil, for God was with him (Acts 10:38). This verse describes Jesus as doing good healing those who were oppressed of the devil. We are to live as Christ lived, casting out demons and also healing all those who are oppressed with the devil. We do not sit by and watch someone being oppressed by the devil, but we are to encourage them and heal them (1 Thessalonians 5:11)! Some people don't believe in deliverance, but its deliverance that saved my soul. It cleansed my seer gift so that I may not be hindered from demonic interference. Demonic interference that may attack seers in this realm can be divination, sorcery, witchcraft; including works of the flesh and perversion. We need deliverance to have a clean scope of what the father is showing us. Not only this, but demons recognize us by our sin and will further antagonize us as a result. For example, if we are suffering with spirits of lust or perversion, the enemy will present an opportunity for you, and if you have not been delivered and are not drenched in the word of God, you will fall victim AGAIN, AND AGAIN AND AGAIN.

Ekballo is the Greek word for cast out.[3] Ekballo also means "to throw out, cast out, banish, expel, drive out, remove, to compel one to depart, draw out with force, tear out, to command, cause one to depart in haste, to reject with contempt." Deliverance is not a violent act, but the intentions are violent for the demons. It may not take one session, sometimes it may take 2, 3, 4, or even much more, depending on the individual person because every situation is different. In Exodus 23:30 God says little and little I will drive them out from before thee, until thou be increased, and inherit the land. God wants us to increase, but we cannot increase until we decrease. There is freedom when we are delivered and demons are cast out of us, however, like a tree that needs to be watered for proper growth, so do we after we are delivered from demonic influence. We need to drench ourselves and immerse ourselves in the father and in his word. In Luke 11:24 it says, "When the unclean spirit is gone out of a man, he walketh through dry places, seeking rest; and finding none, he saith, I will return unto my house whence I came out." When demons are cast out, they will return if we are not properly immersed in prayer daily, immersed in the word. We are to put on the WHOLE ARMOR OF GOD daily and to take up the shield of faith to quench the fiery darts of the enemy (Ephesians 6:10-18). Now is the time to put on your armor, oh WARRIOR!

CHAPTER SEVEN

A Lifestyle Of Holiness And Righteousness

Scriptural base on why we all are called to be holy

The Lord gave me a revelation concerning holiness. According to the scriptures, it's more important for us to walk in righteousness, always being pleasing in the sight our Lord. How can we intercede for others if our heart is not pure? We need pure motives to operate in the gifts the Spirit gives us. When we're living a life that is consistent with the spirit of God, our prophetic flow (utterance) is not contaminated. Contamination only comes from a life not lived in the spirit of God. A life of fasting and daily prayer; praying in the Spirit, singing in the Spirit. WE MUST LIVE A SPIRIT-LED LIFE!

First wash the inside of the cup and the dish, and then the outside will become clean, too". This verse in Matthew 23:26 plays so well with what is being explained concerning "holy". The message conveyed in scripture is not a message of perfection. God's expectations are extremely realistic and attainable. However, the religious laws operating within certain cultures and denominations has made it to be unachievable. However, Spirit-led Hubs, revival centers and churches alike who teach and preach this message, is what challenges the religious systems. Let me just break down the "law" for a moment. The law is very common and what many religions still follow today, and some even completely make up their own, however, to follow some of the law is a sin within it self! you must follow the whole thing! Let's look at Galatians 3:10.

"For all who rely on the works of the law are under a curse, as it is written: "Cursed is everyone who does not continue to do everything written in the Book of the Law." Galatians 2:16: "know that a person is not justified by the works of the law, but by faith in Jesus Christ. So we, too, have put our faith in Christ Jesus that we may be justified by faith in Christ and not by the works of the law, because by the works of the law no one will be justified". Living a life in the flesh is what keeps so many bound and subject to the flesh and therefore remain a slave to sin. Sin is being led by the flesh. But it's the law that makes us realize our sin and that we are sinful, but only through faith in Christ Jesus are we made whole and complete! Let me be very clear concerning what the flesh is exactly: "The acts of the flesh are obvious: sexual immorality, impurity and debauchery; idolatry and witchcraft; hatred, discord, jealousy, fits of rage, selfish ambition, dissensions, factions and envy; drunkenness, orgies, and the like. I warn you, as I did before, that those who live like this will not inherit the kingdom of God" Galatians 5:19-21: Therefore, indulging in these things, is the flesh and being led by the flesh.

We cannot continue pleasing our flesh and feeding its desires. We cannot think for a moment that the Lord will give us anything without first pleasing him! Matthew 6:33 says that we should "seek first the kingdom of God and his righteousness, and all things WILL BE ADDED to you". For quite some time, I have been seeing the manifestations of this scripture. All this verse says is that you place God's mind over what matters to you! "Mind over matter!" When God spoke that to me while in prayer, it made my flesh cringe. So as you can see, my flesh desired what was contrary to the spirit, so my spirit and flesh were in conflict, but because I was led by the spirit and not the law, I was able to submit to what the spirit of God told me. When you live for Christ and allow him to live in you, you can fulfill what he desires for you to do, which is pure workings. God desires us to walk Holy, and he desires us to walk in his righteousness according to Matthew 6:33. I have come to love the scripture in Hebrews 12:14; "make every effort to live in peace with everyone and to be holy; without holiness no one will see the Lord". Holiness is not something we do for ourselves, nor is it temporary. Instead, it's a lifestyle. As I began my transformation, the reason why God changed me from the inside out was so that I can shine his truth, his love, and be an example of his holiness. That's what kingdom is! Religion will tell you that you must work to seek God's approval; going to every single church meeting, cleaning up the church, serving in the church, attending events and venues every month, all this for the sake of pleasing God. Let me just tell you, what I just pointed out needs to come from a heart of SERVING. Remember at the beginning of this book, I explained what it meant to be in Christ and have his heart. It's all about your passion to serve **THE PEOPLE, NOT YOURSELF!**

Taking off our filthy worldly garments and putting on the garments of love, joy, holiness and righteousness. We must not defile ourselves with lusts of the flesh, instead rebuke the flesh.
2 Corinthians 7:1 KJV

"Therefore, since we have these promises, dear friends, let us purify ourselves from everything all filthiness of the flesh and spirit, perfecting holiness in the fear of God."

This verse tells us to clean ourselves from everything of the flesh which is; desires of the world covetousness, and all lusts of the flesh

1 Peter 1:5-16 NIV

"But just as he who called you is holy, so be holy In all you do; for it is written: be holy, because I am holy."

Philippians 214 -16 and NIV

"Do everything without grumbling or arguing so that you may become blameless and pure children of God without fault in a warped and crooked generation then you will shine among them like stars in the sky as you hold firmly to the word of life."

Romans 12:1 NIV

"Therefore I urge you brothers and sisters in view of God mercy to offer your bodies as a living sacrifice holy and pleasing to God this is your true in proper worship."

Colossians 3:8

"But now you also put them all aside anger wrath malice slander and abusive speech from your mouth."

James 3 verse 10

"From the same mouth come both blessing and cursing my

brother these things ought not to be this way."

2 Timothy 2:16

"But avoid worldly and empty chatter for it will lead to further ungodliness."

We must walk in humility daily and renew our minds daily in the word of God. Being a new creature in Christ means your old life has passed away and all things are made new. Walking, thinking and living as Christ, is a constant training field. There is no one person who always has it all together. Romans 12:3 says that we must not think to highly of ourselves than we ought to think. I see and hear too often many saying and bragging about how long they've been saved and somehow being newly saved you cannot know anything, and as if God cannot speak to you without having several years behind you. God does not have a ranking system of who he decides to speak to, instead, "he is no respecter of persons" Romans 2:11. In other words, "God does not play favoritism!". Instead we should be teaching, instructing, and releasing. Getting delivered quickly from spiritual pride before it contaminates your heart. God is raising up apostles and prophets teachers and speakers after his own heart to truly teach and train, release and instruct. Whether you're new or older in Christ, don't fret thyself those matters of the world, God will perfect those things which concerns you, for God has his hands on you and he will never leave you, nor forsake you!!

CHAPTER EIGHT

Heart

Carrying The heart of God

As water reflects the face, so one's life reflects the heart.
Proverbs 27:19

"There is a refining time of authenticity where the Lord takes his time to refine and authenticate us. He will try, polish and shine. Those who rush this process, and not trust the Lord's process, becomes the counterfeit; because they've not adopted the Lord's process but their own, that's the difference" -Misha Wesley

The Heart of a Young Prophet

The deep and inner workings of my heart,

Inside do I hide his word, which does not depart

With weeping and tongues do I praise,

His name is a mighty phrase

My life increases with favor all of my days

To the top of mount Zion do I gaze

In the spirit do I see, all the treasures he has for me

A gold Key to unlock every closed door set before me

A vision into my future through my eyes he let me see

He clothed me in honor and placed upon my head a mantle

Upon my feet I wear fine sandals

Thou shalt increase my greatness and comfort me on every side

In my secret place I cry out, under his wings do i hide

From every oppressor sent my way

God is my strength tho I sing to him night and day

Songs of glory and honor, I shall never bring him dishonor

For he is a good, good father all flesh shall see it together

The joy is not in me but in Christ for he makes me better

My heart cannot hide any longer who he called me to be

His heartbeat do I feel

On my knees do I kneel

His spirit upon me do I feel

The intimacy with GOD is the ultimate deal

Young I am, a novice I am not

With Christ as my teacher I can do all things

Pulling down strongholds and breaking through as I'm trained

A young Prophet I remain....

Submitting to the Lord is hard to do when you are still listening to your own self-will. Your self-will keeps you out of alignment with the Father and out of His heart. The Merriam Webster's dictionary definition for self-will is "a stubborn or willful adherence to one's own desires or ideas"; obstinacy: in Biblical terms, it's your flesh.[4]

Submitting/Submit means to: accept or yield to a superior for or to the authority or will of another person.[5]

In order to see change occur in your life, submission to the Lord is a necessary requirement. In order for deliverance to take place in your life, you must be able to release everything to God and submit yourself to Him. The change I mentioned is necessary for the true advancement and spiritual growth with God. God needs full control of you, and He needs to know that you give Him absolute control of your life: that you have no backup plans; that only the work of His hands can work, and will work, through your struggles, issues and predicaments. Here's another term: Surrender!

Surrender means: to cease resistance to an opponent and submit to their authority[6]. Again, we see the word submit. Some of the mental stress and worry you're still facing is because you're refusing to submit to God's will. When I first fell in love with my husband, I fell deep and hard! I could not help loving those close to me, and I never wanted them to leave me. Throughout my life, I thought carrying such a loving heart was a curse. So I sought to keep people out: building barriers and walls around my heart, knowing if I allow people in, they would realize how soft I was. A former friend told me this would be my downfall, but I knew this couldn't be true of my purpose for this life and why I carried such a loving heart. It is God that taught me to properly guard my heart against predators and people who didn't deserve my heart.

Our Father in heaven loves us unconditionally and deeply. God truly loves us, so much so that He sacrificed His only begotten son so that we may be redeemed (John 3:16). Since childhood, I felt His heart in me, carried His heart, and the love of God favored me, even while I was in darkness. Whenever I look at people now, I see their hearts and the condition it's in. I also see the spirit in operation behind their behavior. This is also known as discernment. But God specifically imparts into us an ability to see into a dimension in which we can see angels. An example of discernment would be the first time I met my husband while in the high school cafeteria, and as we gazed deeply at each other, his heart was screaming for me to love him and his eyes told me, "Help me, I need you!" I couldn't help what I felt his heart scream out to me. Discernment is a deep feeling of knowing something within your spirit. However, discerning of angels would be an ability to see the appearance of angels in a room, building, territory or region. To this day, we are still married and the best of friends!

The heart of a man tells a story of who they are. The heart is the very most intimate part that many try to hide, but prophets are always able to see the heart. I woke up one night out of my sleep and the Holy Spirit said "the heart is treacherous, who can know it? My eyes search the earth for a righteous heart." (Jeremiah 17:9) When I speak of the heart, I speak of what you are in love with, where your heart is consistently stayed on. If the heart and mind is stayed on the things and ways of this world, then your heart will be worldly and filled with carnality. Romans 8:7 says, "Because the carnal mind is enmity against God, for it is not subject to the law of God, neither indeed can be." Therefore, if you are worldly, you are carnal, and if you are carnal, your heart then to is filled with enmity against God. Remember, we may live in this world, but we are not of this world. If then your heart is always stayed on money and obtaining money, then money shall always rule you and you will be a slave to it; your heart is covetous. "For the love of money is the root of all kinds of evil" (1 Timothy 6:10). We all need money and have to have it to pay bills and afford the necessities, but we need to remember God is the one who provides. God is our Jehovah Jireh, our El-Shidah; the God of more than enough!

CHAPTER NINE

The Heart Of Spiritual Warfare

Breakdown of my warfare

Spiritual Warfare is a militant strategy, invoking a battle that takes place in the spirit that we cannot see. Spiritual warfare is a strategy Kingdom warriors use in prayer to battle the enemy; a strategy is key. We may not be able to see the battle, but we sure can feel or discern when it is approaching. "For the weapons of our warfare are not carnal but mighty to the pulling down of strongholds" (2 Corinthians 10:4). Does warfare have a heart? Or could it be God transforming your heart in the midst of spiritual warfare? I looked at this time in my life much like the story of Job. There are events and situations God will allow to happen just to test you, to try you, just to push you. Sounds cruel? On the contrary! In Job 2:1-7 it speaks of God and Satan having a conversation concerning the servant Job.

God did allow Satan to test him, try him, to see if he would curse the name of the Lord in the midst of his trouble and chaos. God allowed Satan to take his possessions including his farmland, animals, children, and even his health! God does allow the battle to intensify, but that is not to be mean. God is a just god and his goal is never to hurt you, but to refine you. However, it's in the middle of your trouble, in the middle of the chaos when we REALLY NEED TO PRAISE GOD all the more. A beautiful scripture I found helpful during spiritual warfare is;

1 Peter 4:12-14
"Beloved, think it not strange concerning the fiery trial which is to try you, as though some strange thing happened unto you. But rejoice, inasmuch as ye are partakers of Christ's sufferings; that, when his glory shall be revealed, ye may be glad also with exceeding joy". I did not love spiritual warfare, but I knew it was a result of me loving Christ and the sense of identity I found through him that the enemy did not like. But I was not facing warfare alone.

God instructed me to go on a strict fast, in which I cut off all contact from anyone and where I buried my head in the Bible and studied, fasted and prayed. Shortly after my fast, God began to reveal a particular friendship in my life that was toxic. Before the Lord revealed this revelation, I had a warning dream about this friendship that led me to prayer and seek the Lord for accuracy in what I saw in the dream: I was walking on a sidewalk and I began to look up at the sky which was blue with beautiful white clouds, and ask the Lord about this friendship. After I asked the Lord, I continued to walk down the sidewalk and make a right turn, then another right turn to walk into a big brown building. I walked down a long dimly lit hallway towards a large room with two brown descending staircases. On one of the descending staircase the friend sat waving so nicely at people as they passed by. She seemed so pleasant and nice as she got up from the staircase, she wore a long old brown dress that resembled what they wore in the 1900's.

She locked arms with me and we proceeded to walk down the hallway together. She knew that I had something to tell her and especially about the way she's been treating me. Since she knew what I was going to say, she immediately yanked her arm from me then began to avenge me! I began to cry with tears streaming down my face asking her why is she like this! She immediately began to lunge this extremely large hard wooden table at me. Before it could touch me, I ran for my life not looking back. But even though I wasn't looking back, I could still feel her rage and anger behind me. Then I woke up.

The Lord exposed through laser sharpened discernment, a contaminated woman in which operated through works of the flesh of control and manipulation. She possessed a calm demeanor outwardly but her heart was critical and condemning. Our conversation of old always left me confused and discouraged, blinded by my lack of spiritual maturity, the spirit within her controlled me and wanted me caged, only to speak as it deems necessary. I discerned a strong spirit of leviathan, Jezebel, and Absalom. This spirit wanted to scare me away from attending my church and eventually, bully me into abandoning seeking after the Lord as hungrily as I did. After breaking away and seeking the Lord, I began to face a raging spiritual battle. During this time, I prayed and continually fasted and became like Anna (Luke 2:36-37). I grew closer and closer with the Lord where I could hear his voice plainly, instructing me and causing me to hearken unto his distinct sound of his voice. During this time I learned to discern the voice of the enemy and of course my own. I received a word from Cal Pierce telling me I was a warrior, likened unto Deborah and that I would never listen to the voice of the enemy. This just confirmed for me that I am a warrior and I shall fight like one! I continued to pray night and day as the spiritual warfare raged, attacks were coming that wanted to cut off my prophetic voice and silence my prayer life. Through this time I never laid my sword down, which is the word of God.

During my rigorous prayer time I was led by the Holy Spirit to rid my home of any foul or hidden spirits. A proper home cleansing is what is needed to prepare it to become permeated with the presence of God. Christ will never dwell in a vessel or place of which is unclean, so I began to cleanse my home using these scriptures:

Psalms 91:1-16 KJV

He that dwelleth in the secret place of the most High shall abide under the shadow of the Almighty. I will say of the Lord, He is my refuge and my fortress: my God; in him will I trust. Surely he shall deliver thee from the snare of the fowler, and from the noisome pestilence. He shall cover thee with his feathers, and under his wings shalt thou trust: his truth shall be thy shield and buckler. Thou shalt not be afraid for the terror by night; nor for the arrow that flieth by day; Nor for the pestilence that walketh in darkness; nor for the destruction that wasteth at noonday. A thousand shall fall at thy side, and ten thousand at thy right hand; but it shall not come nigh thee. Only with thine eyes shalt thou behold and see the reward of the wicked. Because thou hast made the Lord , which is my refuge, even the most High, thy habitation; There shall no evil befall thee, neither shall any plague come nigh thy dwelling. For he shall give his angels charge over thee, to keep thee in all thy ways. They shall bear thee up in their hands, lest thou dash thy foot against a stone. Thou shalt tread upon the lion and adder: the young lion and the dragon shalt thou trample under feet. Because he hath set his love upon me, therefore will I deliver him: I will set him on high, because he hath known my name. He shall call upon me, and I will answer him: I will be with him in trouble; I will deliver him, and honour him. With long life will I satisfy him, and shew him my salvation.

I began to speak these psalms while pleading the blood of Jesus over myself, home, and children. I endured a battle that seemed years long but only lasted a few months. The enemy's camps became the house of Saul and I became like David, growing stronger and stronger. I received another confirming prophetic word from Fred Bennett who had no clue who I was, but yet he said I was on the front lines of battle and that's where I stood.

CHAPTER TEN

The Calling Dream

I was in this house, unsure of who's it was and in the house there was 3 women. We were talking in the living room and then a man pulled up outside. One of the women in the house said, oh no that's my son. Her son seemed demonized when he approached the front door and all three women ran to the front door to keep him out. As they were holding onto the front door keeping the man out, I guarded the back door which I made sure was locked and shut tight. As the women warded off the man and kept him from entering the man stopped. I instructed the women to lock that door and make sure it was closed and she did.

I saw the man try to come around to the back door but obviously he couldn't because I was guarding it and it was locked.

Somehow, I left the door and came by the women to make sure they were okay because they were shrieking after the encounter. As soon as I left the door, the demonized man was able to come in and seems like he brought his family and they all came in. I saw the woman carrying a baby, and I didn't like it. Although the baby wasn't crying, I knew I had to get the baby away from them because they weren't right. Somehow I got the baby, I held it close and began running outside toward my car which was very nice. I got inside the driver seat with the baby and locked the doors. I started the car and was about to drive off when I saw the lady come out to my car and demand the baby back. I opened the door, got out and started speaking to her, I looked her in the eyes and they were gray; but within her eyes I saw a spirit that was not God, it was wicked. I never gave the baby to her, but I told her looking in her eyes that she was not going to harm the baby. As she repeated after me, I saw her body tremble as if she was scared of me.

I saw a demon manifesting within her and I immediately said while laying my hands on her, "In the name of Jesus, Satan I rebuke you!" when I said this, the woman melted away. Then suddenly, the ground began to shake, rocks flew everywhere, then it opened. Out of the ground, rose Satan himself on hind animal legs, he rose big before me. He had the chest of a man, with fur all over his body and great horns like an antelope coming from his head. His face was dark and his eyes were red. Despite Satan standing before me I had no fear. Out of my mouth I told him, "Satan, I rebuke you in the name of Jesus!" He tried to silence me as I said "Jesus" but he was unsuccessful. He reached his fury hand towards me but he didn't touch me because I woke up.

CHAPTER ELEVEN

Breaking Through Hard Ground

Getting breakthrough in prayer

The spirit of leviathan is infiltrating the hearts of man

Pride and anger spreads quickly in a small span

I hear the spirits of pride, violence and murder laughing a taunting shriek

While Jezebel silences the mouths of God's true prophets so they won't speak

These demons are on the rise in our cities and states

While prayerless politicians determine our fate

I can't take this anymore seeing all the violence and bloodshed

My heart is heavy but I refuse to allow in dread

You see there's a higher place in the spirit God has taken me

All spiritual blinders removed now I see

That the enemy uses these as distractions

There is no real war that we can see

But the battle is only won on our knees

The real enemy is Satan that people refuse to see

He uses tricks and tactics to create illusions

Leaving many with religious thoughts and minds clouded with delusion

Put on your whole armor of God oh warrior, let's stand and fight, you shall not be afraid for the terror by night

Many are called but chosen are few, born for greatness and yes God knew

The lord said be of good courage, so I shall not be afraid

For Christ is with me all of my days

Be strong dear heart I'm here to encourage you

For Christ is in me and he's in you too!

Rise up now dry bones I'm commanding you to live!

I declare you live and not die all you Apostles and prophets

There is a calling forth of God's governmental order to throw down religious optics,

Evangelists, teachers rise up too

For evil is at hand we have work to do!!

I realized the intense battle I faced was definitely only the beginning. God began to reveal through prophetic prayer and intercession the plans of the enemy. I began to map out those around me and pray strategically for them. Mapping out someone is truly getting enough information about that person and praying for those specific areas in their life. I prayed for walls to come down; I felt inspired like never before to root out, and to pull down, and to destroy, and to throw down, to build, and to plant (Jeremiah 1:10). We must have a strategy when we pray that is how we overcome and not fall into the wiles of the devil. Wiles are hidden traps, snares, a devious or cunning strategy employed to manipulate. Being fervent and effectual in our prayers avails much (James 5:16). We must also be watchful and vigilant because your adversary the devil walks about like a roaring lion seeking whom he may devour (1 Peter 5:8).

This was the first scripture I memorized as a child; I went through my mother's bible and found this scripture. I believe God was telling me early that I was sent to higher realms in the spirit and also to put on my whole armor of God. As I prayed for my marriage, I began to see so much change in my husband. My prayers for him broke his addictions. I began seeing manifested changes within myself and in my marriage, then I began praying for others. My sister's experienced breakthroughs, as I prayed for their marriage. One of my sister's marriages was actually restored, however, it was short lived as a result of their own disobedience and rebellion. I even began seeing breakthrough at my workplace as I prayed and covered the people and the atmosphere. Restoration was all around me and what's been lost, being found. What would normally take someone years to accomplish through prayer I saw in a couple of days! Immediate change was taking place all around me!

 I never gave up nor did I give in, in fact I grew so close to the Lord he began to illuminate my steps. It was during this time that I developed a bigger heart to serve, to love, a heart to protect and guard. He exposed false friendships, false ministries and false intentions and motives. As I ascended to greater spiritual heights and more mature spiritually, God even began to expose to me conversations people have been having about me, and lies against me were exposed. The closer to God's heart I desired, he began illuminating my calling and that I have been sent.

God revealed his heart for me, his plans for me. It was through prayer he began to speak his mind, his thoughts, his intentions, I felt his heart, and he showed me a glimpse my future. I accepted a position at ADT Security that literally came out of nowhere. I was not actively looking for employment when they called me and invited me to interview with them. I was still working a current position processing loans, a position I have held for the last 3 years. As I interviewed for the position, the GM was so impressed with my energy he hired me on spot. He told me that no one he knew had such an energetic energy and looked so bright. Now I'm a dark skin woman, not really light, but I knew this brightness he referred to had nothing to do with my skin tone but it was Christ that dwelled in me.

I spent the majority of my one-hour lunch breaks praying and sacrificed eating food for eating the word of God. This particular afternoon, I was burdened for the loss of lives as result of a shooting where Caucasian police officers and African Americans lost their lives. After lunch, I sat in the training room waiting for my GM to come back from lunch so we can finish training. I began writing and breaking down a scripture that popped into my mind. As I was writing, I looked up from my paper and gazed lightly over the board filled with ADT material. At the top of the board read "ADT Security," then off to the side I saw in plain sight, "intercessor and prophetess." I thought I was imagining things because I blinked and shook my head and they disappeared. I shook it off and continued writing, then I heard the Holy Spirit say, "you are my prophetess, you are to protect and guard the people, you are to secure lives and homes in the natural and in the spiritual."

His words didn't scare me, but calmed. Of anything I was nervous cause of the load and burden of the office of the prophet.

Later I cried out to god asking how he could choose me and I was not worthy. I asked him to confirm his words and show me how to walk boldly and courageously.

My husband and I attended a John Eckhardt conference in Olive Branch, MS. That is where I met a wonderful sister in Christ. She sat behind me and all I kept hearing from God was Fire. I was wondering what this meant. Maybe a fire in the hallway, but I didn't smell smoke. I shook it off and continued listening to the preaching. Later John Eckhardt decided to do a small activation where each person in one row would give the person behind them one word they heard God saying to them or they believed God was giving them for that person. The word I heard was the word for this woman, but as I looked in her eyes, I also heard water. But I was obedient to give her the one word. Later, he said that we are to prophesy off of that one word and give them a full word. This made me so joyful as God already gave me exactly what to prophesy. Later she confirmed my word the next morning and how joyful and excited she was for me delivering that on time word. We prayed together on many occasions and as we prayed I began seeing miracles take place in my life and in hers. She was led on a particular day to pray for me, still not knowing much about me. she prophesied a strong word over my life and confirmed my calling and that I was set in the office of the Prophet.

I found that I had to travel away for training to another state and I was not sure of where they would place me. They choose to send me to Dallas, TX in the midst of the shooting that had taken place. The revelation did not come to me that I was sent on assignment until that Sunday night I was getting ready for bed. The Lord instructed me carefully, I am to discern the territory and pray over the land. In fact, the hotel I stayed at was 10 minutes from where John F Kennedy was assassinated and from where the shootings actually took place. I really cannot make this stuff up! God truly sent me onto that land! As I walked around the hotel, I kept smelling a pungent type of smell, it didn't stink but it was like almost a hidden type of smell, meaning I had to smell it with my spirit. The Holy Spirit revealed to me that it was a spirit of Obscurity in this land which means, this spirit did not want to be noticed and it wanted to stay hidden. I discerned a strong territorial spirit over that region that was separation, and confusion, anger and much hostility. This was all the fruit of a Leviathan Spirit.

I prayed during the 1st and 2nd watch primarily between the hours of 6pm-9pm and from 9pm to 12pm. I didn't know why I prayed on these particular times, I just did. I later found out these prayer watches are very strategic for breaking down barriers and walls of the enemy. The first watch is from 6pm to 9pm and called the apostolic watch. It was during this watch when Jesus went off to pray and spend time with the Father. It is also a time for deep reflection from the chaos of the day. During the 2nd watch, from 9pm to 12pm is the midnight watch. On this watch, intercessors are able to impact the spiritual realm before the enemy begins to wreak havoc. In the natural this is a time of darkness but in the spirit, it's a time where the enemy begins to set demonic plots and schemes into motion. On this watch we can break the plans and attacks of the enemy before they occur. It was on this watch is where I usually did my binding and loosing and crying out for Dallas. I was not from Dallas, nor I have I ever been there before, but in the spirit, being from a place does not matter, Because I was sent from God with authority to bind and loose and I had a heart to guard and protect. At the end of my journey, I met a wonderful woman that I was drawn to. She was a native Texan and carried such a bright light of Christ. After prophesying that I saw Christ drawing young people to her and her being surrounded by young people and she would be the light of Christ and people from young to old would be drawn to her. After giving her that word and her receiving what Christ showed me, she confirmed that she has an outreach youth ministry and goes to Gateway church in Dallas TX.

We connected and still are friends till his day. I had the pleasure of prophesying to another woman of God in my training class. For the entire duration of class, I continuously heard God speaking to me about a particular woman in my class. There was not enough information from God to prophesy a word over her, nor did I feel the strong bubbling unction to. On the last day of class, God finally gave me the entire word for her and I pulled her to the side and began prophesying and ministering the word. Tears welled up in her eyes as I clothed her with the armor of God, setting first upon her head the helmet of salvation. She was a warrior, so I had to prophesy strength and protection over and her family. After setting the word and prophesying, she told me babies always look at her as if there is something on her head as well as people; she thanked me and also stated she has never received a word that was so powerful that made her cry! I left which blessed me to give more than to receive!

On the plane ride back to Memphis, I sat by the window and looked down at the ground. I beheld the beauty of the land at 30,00 feet. I marveled such a creation looking down at the rivers that seemed to form figures of angels. The thick white puffy clouds resembled God's kingdom, all his might and majesty. I relished the scenery and my heart grew ever the more, never cursing again the heart I carried because I knew this heart was God's. Tears began to stream down my face as I accepted being sent and accepted my calling. No more fearing what people thought about me, and that I would do it all for God. It was at this time where I fell in love with God's people and his creation so much more that I promised the Lord I will accept my assignment and walk boldly in my calling for such a time as this.

CHAPTER TWELVE

Your Ministry Begins Right Where You Are!

You are your ministry; it starts with you and those around you

For though I preach the gospel, I have nothing to glory of: for necessity is laid upon me; yea, woe is unto me, if I preach not the gospel!! 1 Corinthians 9:16

Wherever you are Christ wants us to minister, speak and preach the gospel of Christ. In love we are to minister; not out of fear, but we are to captivate other non-believers and draw them in with love and show of Christ working through us! We cannot force anyone's hand, nor can we beat them down with condemnation, but we are to allow our light to shine so bright for all to see, that other may see your good works and glorify your Father which is in heaven (Matthew 5:16). When I use to work for the loan company, God revealed this time would be the perfect training ground. I encountered many people under the control of oppression, fear, anxiety, trauma, hurt, and deep pain.

I was able to move in the gifting of discerning of spirits. Discerning of spirits is a gifting that comes straight from God himself and is more intensified than discernment. In fact, as I drove to work one morning, I began to pray in tongues without stopping until I got to work. I don't usually do this, but I was led by the spirit to do so. As I approached my work building, in the spirit I saw a monstrous Octopus, hideous-looking and sitting on top of the building! I looked, but wasn't terrified; instead my tongues grew louder and stronger and I directed my prayers toward the Octopus and soon, its tentacles unsuctioned from around the building and lifted up and away! The octopus is a mind-controlling demon among other ocean-dwelling spirits.

Ocean-dwelling demons symbolize the depths of the soul. Usually these demons are deeply entrenched in one's mind and psyche. Our eyes should only be windows for what Jesus Christ desires us to see. At that particular time, Holy Spirit allowed me to see this octopus because he wanted me to guard (Shamar), and protect (Shamar) the place that I worked. Holy Spirit used my workplace to strengthen me in the area of guarding and protecting prayer. The mission as God gave me the grace, was to pray for all the people that came and sat at my desk. I prayed with a woman that was stricken with the spirit of fear. I talked to her and through the conversation she revealed to me the terror she lives in. Fearful for her children leaving for college and leaving her alone, fearful of falling in love, fearful of even the word of God, praying and worshipping. The spirit of fear convinced her so much that the word of God was spooky and worship was scary! However, we know that in 2 Timothy 1:7 God did not give us the spirit of fear, but he gave us POWER, LOVE and a SOUND MIND.

This fear comes from the evil one. Understand people, we are called to be courageous, bold as a lion, our faith steadfast and unmovable! After conversing with her a little more, she became so comfortable and settled. As I ministered to her and explained with love who Christ is and how he can take away all her fears. she became so soft and feeble like she wanted to know more. As I finished processing the loan, I asked to pray with her. As I prayed with her, she began to cry and sob. She told me she was not expecting to be prayed with today. Many of the people that came to me had heavy, deep-rooted problems and after they left my desk, I gave them a little of Christ. I remember calling a man on the phone that had a delinquent account. He was really upset that I called but the more he spoke, I could hear through his voice he was stricken with pain. I dug deeper to see why he couldn't pay his loan. He became comfortable and broke down and said, "you're the only one that bothers to care. Honestly,

I just lost my mother". I told him I was sorry for his loss and prayed with him. He was extremely surprised. He explained that he would be up to the office first thing in the morning. I know better not to believe everybody that tells me stories, but with the help of Christ and the gift of discernment, I heard something deeper for that customer.

The next day, the man came up to the office looking for me. He came and approached my desk and thanked me for taking time out to care. I told him it was my pleasure. He told my boss that no one cared he lost his mom but me. It was the tools Christ gave me that helped me to understand why he was acting that way and it was Christ that allowed me to minister perfectly. I had a heart for prayer and I loved seeing people free of worry and anguish. I would often teach my coworkers and pray for them and with them. They had many questions and because Christ was working through me, I answered a lot of their questions. My boss became very close to me as a result of me ministering to him. I loved my little work family because they knew and saw my love; it allowed them to be friendly and loving back.

I talked to my mother, sisters and brother all the time about Christ and how he transformed me and they have been transformed as a result of my teaching. I spoke to a woman that asked me to pray for her on different occasions. I obediently helped and truly ministered to her with love. I prayed deep prayers with her on several occasions and even received breakthrough in her own marriage. I was getting through to her, but unfortunately, one day, she instead chose the underworld instead of Christ. Self-will is what will keep us from obeying the Father and without a submitted and surrendered life we will fall victim to the hands of the enemy. You can be on as many prayer lines and receive a million prophetic words for direction, but that cannot grow and mature your relationship with the father. God is relational, and he wants an intimate marriage and covenant with you. You must pray and press in for yourself! Do not allow your self-will to keep YOU FROM BEING OBEDIENT TO GOD!

It hurts me even now to write this because she began instead to despise me. I never gave up, but I did place my prayers in God's hands and waited for him to return her heart to him and when she does turn her life over to Christ, he would be there to give her more love than she ever felt in this ENTIRE WORLD! I had a dream about her in which God showed me myself in a house and out of the window, I looked out and saw her. God began to tell me that her heart was filled with strife and she carried a murderous heart. He then showed me myself on a phone as I was driving in my car on one occasion and talking with her. He told her, that her ways are far from him, and whatever she does with her hands will not prosper Because she refused to heed the voice of the prophet and turn away from destruction.

When I woke up, I wanted to call her and tell her but God stopped me. I even called her up on the phone as she prepared to go to a job interview that morning. God stopped my words so much, I could not get them out! That was God's way of telling me, enough talking and wait for him. I have learned throughout this journey, enduring his chastening and yielding to Holy Spirit that the one who plants is nothing, and neither he that waters; but it is God that gives the increase (1 Corinthians 3:7).

CHAPTER THIRTEEN

Spirit

WHO AM I? WHAT DO I DO?

Who am I, but a mere servant of the Lord. Sitting and waiting at his gates.

Who am I, but a lover of ALL THE THINGS OF GOD and despise the ways of the world.

Who am I, but a believer in Christ, a worshiper, intercessor, and a watchman in front of the gates of the City!

What do I do, but work for the Lord, I prophesy, speaking words of the learned for a mantle I've earned,

What do I do, But Dreaming dreams and much visions,

interpreting by inspiration of the holy spirit it's really not my decision.

Who am I to think I can carry the Lord's heart and see the way I do? But it's only Jesus who told me to.

I can't help who I am, I stand out instead of fitting in, without even trying I'm an oddball maybe the reason is what's within.

I know I am young but a Novice I am not

This is who I was created to be from the start

Who am I to have this heart, that loves so hard

Who am I and what do I do, but Serve the Lord IN ALL THAT I DO!

CHAPTER FOURTEEN

The River Of The Prophetic

The atmosphere that grooms the prophetic gift

He that believeth on me, as the scripture hath said, out of his belly shall flow rivers of living water. John 7:38

"The prophetic is a river, and the river is the life of the prophetic, the word of God breeds knowledge and understanding into the Prophetic"

MY LETTER TO JESUS

Oh, Jesus I love you! Why wouldn't I serve you with my life??!! You are my life! The price you paid for my life on the cross means that my life was bought at a price. The shedding of your innocent blood is the perfect sacrifice. There is no man like you; I know that I've fallen head over heels in love. My heart bears your burdens, I grieve what you grieve, I see what you see and believe as you believe, speak as You speak teach as you teach and walk holy and righteous as you taught. You are the light of the world and in me is you and your spirit is true. I see no other reason why I should not place you above all things, serving you with my life as I worship the father in spirit and in truth. You are lord of lords and king of kings, the glory of your cross reigns supreme! I am but a servant to you and to the world of hopelessness. Infilling in them what you have put in me which is complete freedom and truth! The true gifts of the spirit to speak in tongues, activate and impart. Your wisdom you placed in me, shall never depart!

I fell in love with the word of God and in love with every word the scriptures held. The word of God became my bread day and night. I studied to shew thyself approved (2 Timothy 2:15) and when I say this, I truly mean it. I would read the scriptures and desire to walk them out, teach them, preach them, lead through them. I studied them so much I compared versions, studied and researched concepts and biblical history. I literally became obsessed with God and wanted to be with him all the time in prayer. God wants us to fall in love with him and be submerged into his presence. I fell in love with God over and over and over again. The love and intimacy I feel for Christ and him dying for my sins is the ultimate sacrifice! My heart swells for the prophetic and I coveted to prophesy. To covet something, means you yearn to possess it or to have it.[7]

I sought to prophesy and did not desire or covet the things of this world. To covet something means to yearn to possess or to have it really bad[5]; but we can covet to prophesy and desire spiritual gifts all day long according to 1 Corinthians 14:39. I desired to be better than my former self. I was on Facebook one day and I saw a post one of my friends shared, and it was a post of John Eckhardt teaching on the subject of the prophetic. I began following the teaching of this man of God and following him on periscope as he prayed for the 50 states of America. Because I was in love with the prophetic already, I felt he blessed my life evermore through his teaching and supernatural impartation. A supernatural impartation is when gifts from God get placed within you without the laying on of hands. In other words, you receive it by faith.

I am a firm believer of supernatural impartation because as a result of his teaching, preaching, prophesying and endless teaching on Youtube and activations, I am stronger and flow smoothly in this area. I was speaking to a young lady about being aligned with an Apostle as opposed with a pastor, or preacher. Not that anything is wrong with pastors and preachers I love them. We all love them. However, being aligned with the right apostolic leader helps us to better understand our calling in ministry, our direction in ministry, they help teach us, release us and equip us for the calling that God placed on our lives. It's imperative as a prophet of the most High God, that I am aligned spiritually with a strong apostolic covering that can watch my growth and development spiritually, challenge me and groom me to be better. I feel as a prophet we cannot be lone rangers, wandering without a covering. Rebellion can plague anybody, especially prophets, and Spiritual protection for God's people depends completely upon proper positioning. The Power of Prayer is one key area that allows us covering as I explained in previous chapters. It's through my prayers, decrees and covering my family with the Blood of Jesus Christ, that all the people around me were protected and safe from harm of the evil one.

Another example is Divinely appointed relationships. Divine relationships are those relationships God uses and appoints, to allow proper grooming, maturing and better spiritual health. "Then the LORD will provide shade for Mount Zion and all who assemble there. He will provide a canopy of cloud during the day and smoke and flaming fire at night, covering the glorious land. It will be a shelter from daytime heat and a hiding place from storms and rain" Isaiah 4:5-6. In verse 5, "Then the LORD will provide shade for Mount Zion and all who assemble there", this is the actual churches, the assemblies of God.

I praise the Lord that he is raising up Apostolic and prophetic leaders in this season that are truly after the heart of

God. We must make it our mission to get into an environment and around a company of Prophets and prophetic leaders that stirs up our gifts, our worship, our prayer lives, challenges us to be better and to lead more holy and righteous lives. We must be around other prophetic people and prophets because it's to my knowledge and according to scripture when we get around other prophetic people, it is definitely contagious!

1 Corinthians 14:1, in the KJV, it says, "Follow after charity and desire spiritual gifts, but rather that ye may prophesy." The King James version states that we should desire spiritual gifts, but the true gift is the Holy Spirit and you should know that in the original translation gifts was not in there. Instead the NLT says, "Let love be your highest goal! But you should also desire the special abilities the Spirit gives--especially the ability to prophesy." This scripture allows us to know that the Holy spirit is the one who gives us special abilities and we should desire to prophesy. A desire is a desperate need to have, to lust after with the heart. God wants us to desire and lust to prophecy and for the spiritual gifts. There are diversities of gifts, but the same spirit and there are differences of administrations but the same Lord (1 Corinthians 14:4,5). The gifts of the spirit are wisdom, knowledge, faith, healing, the workings of miracles, the gift of prophecy, discerning of spirits, divers kinds of tongues and the gift of interpretation of tongues.

The prophetic is a river, and the river is the life of the prophetic, the word of God breeds knowledge and understanding into the Prophetic. Prophecy is a river that flows from your belly. A figurative river that can only be seen and observed with spiritual eyes. I first began moving in the prophetic realm as I joined my Apostolic Center; CITY GATE. When I joined the worship, it was unlike anything I have never seen nor have experienced. The atmosphere was glorious, and I felt free. Free to be who I wanted and free to sing and dance. We didn't just sing a good song from an old hymn book and sit down, not that there's anything wrong with doing that but we really pressed into the spirit of God, waiting for the spirit of the lord to come strongly. "Because where the spirit of the lord is there is freedom" 2 Corinthians 3:17. As we press in and worship singing the songs of the Lord, we allowed the word of God to Nataph which is a Hebrew word meaning to drop, let drop, to prophesy[8]! My Apostle Clay Nash would rise up and prophesy, others would stand up and prophesy as well. When the presence of God is welcomed into worship, it allows his word to build up then drop onto us while in service. As the word drops, it falls like rain onto his prophetic people and we prophesy by the unction of the spirit one by one. This atmosphere was extremely conducive to my growth in the prophetic and developing a strong flow just like a river.

When the Lord puts his word in my mouth, I operate more Nabiy[9] than anything. This is a Hebrew Word meaning "to bubble forth, like a fountain"; the word flows out of me, I announce or pour forth the declarations of God. The word in me becomes like a pot of boiling water, building up to its hottest point and bubble forth. When I feel the unction to prophesy to someone God tells me to speak to, the word becomes so strong and I am compelled by his hand to deliver that word. I was at the gas station waiting in line to pay for gas. In front of me stood this tall heavy muscle-built man. For some reason I could only look at his legs which were large and massive. Then I heard the Lord say "I shall trample upon the lion and adder: the young lion and dragon thou shalt trample under foot", Psalms 91:13. Then I saw him in the spirit literally stepping on these creatures with these massive legs. In the spirit I saw him carrying armor upon his back. As I went back to my car, I felt the strong unction and the word bubbling up in my belly to prophesy to him. I stood by my car and contemplated not to, then the Lord said if you don't, you'll be disobedient to my instruction. Not wanting to be disobedient to my father, I called to the man and immediately delivered the word. Turned out he was an MMA fighter for a living and literally fought in real life. He told me he was Hebrew and that the word was a blessing and on time. It doesn't matter whether we be Jews or Gentiles, whether we be bond or free, we have been all made to drink into one spirit, 1 Corinthians 12:13.

The prophetic is the God encounter America needs; it's the encounter we've all been waiting for. Because the prophetic is not just some person's belief about your life but it is truly from the Holy Spirit. In the last days, God says, "I will pour out my Spirit upon all people. Your sons and daughters will prophesy. Your young men will see visions, and your old men will dream dreams (Acts 2:17)". God wants ALL PEOPLE TO PROPHESY, and God has ALREADY POURED OUT HIS SPIRIT! If you have ever been in John Eckhardt's' prophetic activations, you can truly sense the strong presence of the Holy spirit and the atmosphere as there are almost thousands of people prophesying over one another. When I say that the prophetic is a God encounter, I mean we can hear the words that God is saying to us specifically. As they listen, their secret thoughts will be exposed, and they will fall to their knees and worship God, declaring, "God is truly here among you" 1 Corinthians 14:25. All the scriptures are prophetic and the prophetic is what speaks the heart, the will, and the intentions of God. You become his mouthpiece. Then the LORD reached out his hand and touched my mouth and said to me, "I have put my words in your mouth", Jeremiah 1:9. when you enter into the prophetic realm, your river begins to flow stronger and stronger with every utterance. But it takes faith to strengthen that flow. For without faith it is impossible to please God, Hebrews 11:1. To move in the gifts of the spirit takes courage, boldness and faith and without these, our gifts will lay stagnant, and dormant. Living in the spirit is what purifies us and walking in righteousness and holiness brings us closer to god and worthy enough to be his mouthpiece. We are all spirit beings and to have a pure prophetic utterance. We cannot live in the flesh because the flesh was crucified on the cross when Jesus died, Mark 15:25. He died in the flesh and rose from the dead on the 3rd day, and lives in the spirit which resides in us.

Praying in Tongues.

I want to elaborate on the subject of speaking in tongues. There was a time in which I was unable to speak in other languages or in diversities of tongues as the Apostle Paul states in the book of Corinthians. However, I desired God so much, my hunger for him grew to astronomical levels. All I wanted was his word and everything he wanted to offer me. My husband's cousin was very encouraging and told me I needed to ask earnestly for the gift and our father would give. At that time in my life, I was extremely surprised that God would give such a beautiful utterance to me so quickly without me doing anything in return. He is a God that gives freely! Praying in tongues are mysteries to men but a clear line of communication to The Father, 1 Corinthians 14:2. When we speak to him in our heavenly language, The Holy Spirit takes control of our tongue and then begins praying the PERFECT PRAYER. The enemy cannot understand what we say, some people cannot understand either, unless they interpret what the tongues say. Now if you have not received this wonderful gift from the Holy Spirit, do not fret thyself any longer, but instead ask the Father who gives to each one of us diligently as we ask. Speaking in tongues is a clear line of communication to the father. There is a gift of interpretation of tongues that God has graced to many and God has graced me to carry this gift of interpretation.

In Acts 2:4 everyone present in the room became filled with the Holy Spirit and began speaking in tongues (New Living Translation calls it, "other Languages") So on the day of Pentecost, which came 50 days after the Passover, when Jesus was crucified, all the Apostles were filled with the Spirit of Christ, which is his Holy Spirit or Holy Ghost (same thing), and all spoke in tongues. If you have been baptized (Born again) YOU CAN SPEAK IN TONGUES! Psychologically, when we speak in tongues, there is a part of our brain that relaxes and literally calms. A Neuroscientific study from the University of Pennsylvania as well as Reports from the New York Times, has been done on five women, as they spoke in tongues and sang prophetic songs. According to their research, as they spoke in tongues and found that their frontal lobes — the thinking, willful part of the brain through which people control what they do — were relatively quiet, as were the language centers. The regions involved in maintaining self-consciousness were active. The women were not in blind trances, and it was unclear which region was driving the behavior. I love when science backs up what God does within us that cancels out the voices of all the naysayers and critical spirits in the world! These are quite astounding evidence that reveals God's abilities and strength, therefore, I assure you it is not spooky or weird, but powerful!

CHAPTER FIFTEEN

The Push And Release

My birthing and releasing

After receiving the position at ADT Security and the Lord placing the revelation in my heart of who I am, God began to confirm the calling from the mouths of many witnesses; through prophecy, people in the streets, at work, and from my sister in Christ. God strategically put into place many people to confirm that I was his Prophet. At first I did not want to accept this calling, or office. I knew that carrying such a mantle meant heavy responsibility and if anyone knows me, I am one of those people that take responsibility extremely seriously. Anything I am entrusted with I carry out with excellence and honor until its full completion. I knew this office carried all that and more, and that was why I was wavering. I feel those who truly are called to the office never have to announce themselves as prophet. Heaven recognizes your name.

Then it is heaven that releases your name into the earth so all can know and confirm the calling of God on your life. Then, Hell knows your name, hence the intense warfare a prophet endures. When I first met my sister in Christ, we barely knew each other, but we were speaking life over one another. She prophesied over me when I barely even knew her. She poured onto me a strong prophetic word in which made me fall on my face! After several confirmations from many people, I finally accepted the calling on my life and stepped over the threshold into the office. As I took position as watchmen and as God's Shamar Prophet, there was certain foods I had to put down, certain prayer watches I became acclimated to praying on. The lifestyle changes God did within me began to spill over into my waking life. My husband began to take keen notice of the deep lifestyle changes as well as the deeply rooted spiritual changes within my heart.

As the Lord began increasing within me, I began to become sharpened when I met My sister in Christ; she lived in a complex where every single address began with the number 10. Till this day I see the repetitive numbers 10:10 everywhere; at work and in newspapers. The number ten is a significant number and a governmental number identifying the law of God. In the Gospel of John, Jesus says the words, "I am" exactly 10 times, Luke 17:11-19, Jesus cleanses ten lepers, we are to tithe 10% of our income. In Exodus 12:3 the Passover Lamb was to be sacrificed on the 10th day of the month. Shortly after seeing the number 10, I began seeing the number 12 everywhere I go. I actually was offered a new position (I LOVED by the way) in which I started on the 12th day of the 9th month, and I work on the 12th floor of the building. I was born in the 12th month of the year and like the number ten, this is an apostolic number and also governmental. The number 12 is a perfect number symbolizing God's power and authority as well serving as a perfect governmental foundation. There were 12 disciples that walked with Jesus in which they were taught and trained by Christ, on the day of Pentecost, the Holy spirit fell on all the disciples in the upper room in Acts 2.

The Holy Spirit revealed to me while I was in prayer 3 different books. I asked God this question, "If I am to be your prophet, illuminate which character in your word am I most like? And when you reveal this to me how can I learn from that character?" Opening the book it fell on the book of 2 Kings and the 1st chapter. I then closed the book and opened it, it fell on the book of Joshua. I closed it once more, and it fell open again to the book of 2 Kings and the 1st chapter. This is not just a coincidence, because I asked with my heart and I believed in him for an answer and the Holy Spirit revealed to me who I was and how I should learn from the prophets Elijah, Elisha, and Joshua. The prophets Elijah and Elisha did not just prophecy, but they prophesied with governmental authority. Elijah and Elisha, exemplifies the prophet's ministry of setting and declaring God's order. Meaning that when they prophesied, it was truly the word of God and when they prophesied the words surely did come to pass, meaning that it happened!!

There is more to the office of the prophet than just prophesying and seeing into the spirit realm. Jesus himself chooses and appoints the ones to be prophets, we are set in the church to help and serve in the church. God showed me very soon after Holy Spirit gave me the confirmation of Elijah, Elisha, and Joshua, only this time, He showed me more plainly in a dream. In this dream, I heard his voice, still and calm. The dream was simple and in this dream, God had me write as he spoke. On notebook paper, I took notes on exactly what he said. He broke down to me the number 12 and the repetitive reasons why I saw it. God had me write on a sheet of notebook paper as I listened to his voice and this is exactly how I saw it;

The number 12

Law/Government

Governmental Prophet

Order

Your marital anniversary was my law and government

(This actually is very personal to me because it relates to when my husband and I was married; 10/10)

CHAPTER SIXTEEN
The Set Up For It All!

This season in my life is very personal, however, I desire for you to take a look at how God will announce his Prophet and lay out his ORDER without us pushing our way through. The Lord showed up and showed out today in a magnificent way. The service shifted to a worship atmosphere. Suddenly, the speaker was prophesying over the congregation and telling us what she sees. The heavens were open by this time and the angels were ministering all over bringing messages and decrees to the Lord. she then spoke again what she saw happening. At this time, some people were out of their seats and taking communion and repenting, weeping, and singing songs of the lord. She then said that she saw a book, a giant book coming through the atmosphere and it's coming from this house. My heart, knowing God was speaking specifically to me. She said "this book will change lives."

Then Apostle Clay Nash began to pray over this book, for the writer and for him to receive this book. He asked God to prepare his heart for it. I began weeping uncontrollably as he prayed, and as everyone touched in agreement. As I stood up, I felt the warmth of the father's hand on my shoulder. He prayed that this book not sit on the shelves but it will sell! I came to him crying and carrying my little girl in my arms who was 11 months. I told him that I held back telling him about this book and I was weeping as I told him the title. As I looked at him, for a moment I froze looking into his eyes and seeing a heart filled with so much genuine love, I mean a true earnest type of love. His eyes were telling me to calm down and to breathe. He decided then to pray over me, commission in agreement regarding this book; that it will be finished and it will touch lives!

Jesus sets the stage, and all we do is relax and allow him to come into us. We do not go about flaunting who we are or manipulating to make room for yourself, but instead your gift will make room for you and your gift that God places inside you will bring you before great men! Proverbs 18:16. But God wants to see your heart first. A true repenting heart, a true giving and loving heart. Something my pastor always says is to just BE YOU! Don't bother being anyone else but you. Seek God daily and seek to cleanse your hearts.

My dear brothers and sisters

It is my goal and mission to see the body of Christ functioning in its full capacity. My vision and desire is to see all the members of the body functioning in their rightful place. One of the main reasons people leave a ministry is because they have no place or feel out of place. We have forgotten them! And we have forgotten the most important aspect of the KINGDOM which is to SERVE!

The fivefold is to TEACH:
Holiness and righteous living; no more compromising and mixing the beliefs of the world with kingdom principles. Teach the word of God and teach the rest of the body HOW to apply these principles, TRAIN:
in the area of deliverance, in the area of the PROPHETIC; prophetic activations, prophetic presbytery, the reason God made ALL to be PROPHETIC is because we ALL should HEAR from GOD! The prophetic is God's word and to fall in love with the prophetic is to fall in love with GOD'S WORDS! Now, if you put a lid on the prophetic, YOU WILL SURELY PUT A LID ON THE GROWTH OF YOUR MINISTRY!
Finally, ACTIVATE!

To activate is to get one moving in that realm of deliverance, of being an effective seer, or prophesying. That's how the body can grow and expand! Consider a doctor, before a doctor can operate on ANYONE and especially before they can have their own practice, they must be approved and cleared, as well as become board certified. Not only this, but they undergo a battery of testing.

God is the one who approves and clears those whom he has chosen to teach, to train and to activate. He will send those battery of tests, however, he has deposited in each person a purpose, a destiny, dreams and hopes. Too many are walking around in the body, undiscovered and lost. Leaders have either became fearful of those they shepherd and won't release them.
Leviathan has gripped the hearts of man, allowing them to operate in ignorance of God's warnings and not training and activating those he has sent himself into that leaders care. Like a patient and doctor relationship, you are under the care of your leader and if your doctor is not administering the care you deserve, that patient will seek out another doctor. Now, i am not speaking about those who leave under false pretenses, because they need deliverance and their issue is a heart issue. I am speaking of those sheep who wait patiently!

This is the season of those kingdom leaders rising that WILL love to see his KINGDOM ADVANCE! These new leaders will go out into the world and make disciples of many! These new leaders have emerged from the pits of training where they've battled and slayed giants when NO ONE SAW! The world is SHIFTING INTO PLACE causing many young Apostolic leaders and prophetic voices to emerge! Now is the time when we will hear of many fresh voices we've never heard of come out with the knowledge of only God's kingdom!
No more I declare and decree, as long as I have a breath in me and baptized in the blood of Christ, shall I go about just

WATCHING the condition of the body suffer!

It's MANDATE SEASON!

GO!

For thus saith the lord in the last days, I shall pour out my spirit upon all flesh and your sons and daughters shall prophesy Joel 2:28

For there are many of you reading this right now that are full of many spiritual gifts, many of you have double anointing from the father.

God has graced you, God has gifted you and god has placed you here for such a time as this!

But god has told me in a dream that you must get out of that place you have been stuck in! There are people out there that need your gifts, they need your anointing!

God said stop allowing your gifts to lay dormant.

Many of you can teach, preach, prophesy, cast out devils and I give you authority to do so in my name, but you chose not to!

Woe unto those who do not preach the gospel! 1 Corinthians 9:16

God said do not allow fear to keep you from prophesying, stop allowing fear to keep you from activating, stop allowing fear to keep you from teaching and training and releasing!

For it takes faith to move mountains, faith to prophesy, faith to teach, faith to cast out devils, faith to activate individuals, and faith to preach!

You have been anointed for such a time as this, so stop waiting and GO!

In Jesus' Name, Amen.

About The Author

Raised as a Muslim for the majority of my childhood, there was not much for a young girl to be in that religion. Therefore, aspiring to do anything with my life other than raising children. I have always loved writing, but I have never imagined it as a career choice until after my father died when I was just 11 years old. Before he died, he converted to Christianity. Still grieved with sadness and a heavy heart, I took to writing more and more. Writing has always been my outlet of how I escaped my current impoverished living conditions. Even though my father converted to Christianity, I didn't fully give my life to Christ until later in my late teens. It was then, the Lord led me through deliverance from religious bondage and the trauma I encountered as a child, which opened the door for the enemy.

My greatest passion that Jesus deposited in me is to purge the body of Christ and bring deliverance, which is genuine healing. To teach the body of Christ the true kingdom mission, and the true word of God. My burning passion is to train and equip them to know how all believers in Christ can walk in authority as Kingdom citizens, and release the power of God to reach eventually every non-believer and believer on a global scale! The kingdom of God is forever growing and it is my mandate to help the kingdom ADVANCE! So in this place I write to you, my brethren, telling my story of hope, love, and how I overcame by the blood of Jesus Christ.

Order Additional Copies Today!

Go to www.republishing.org

References

1. vagabond. (n.d.). Dictionary.com Unabridged. Retrieved June 13, 2017 from Dictionary.com website http://www.dictionary.com/browse/vagabond

2. G4982 - sōzō - Strong's Greek Lexicon (KJV). Retrieved from https://www.blueletterbible.org//lang/lexicon/lexicon.cfm?Strongs=g4982&t=kjv

3. G1544 - ekballō - Strong's Greek Lexicon (KJV). Retrieved from https://www.blueletterbible.org//lang/lexicon/lexicon.cfm?Strongs=g1544&t=kjv

4. "Obstinacy." Merriam-Webster.com. Merriam-Webster, n.d. Web. 6 June 2017.

5. "Submit." Merriam-Webster.com. Merriam-Webster, n.d. Web. 6 June 2017.

6. "Surrender." Merriam-Webster.com. Merriam-Webster, n.d. Web. 6 June 2017.

7. "Covet." Merriam-Webster.com. Merriam-Webster, n.d. Web. 13 June 2017.

8. H5197 - nataph - Strong's Hebrew Lexicon (KJV). Retrieved from. https://www.blueletterbible.org//lang/lexicon/lexicon.cfm?Strongs=h5197&t=kjv

9. H5030 - nabiy' - Strong's Hebrew Lexicon (KJV). Retrieved from https://www.blueletterbible.org//lang/lexicon/lexicon.cfm?Strongs=h5030&t=kjv

Index

A

abomination, 10
activations, 56, 69, 73
addictions, 23, 54
agreement, 4, 25, 82
Allah, 11, 14
angels, 41, 59, 81
anointing, 2, 85
apostles, 25, 36, 53, 69, 75
armor, 30, 52, 54, 58, 73
authority, 3, 11, 39–40, 58, 79, 85, 87

B

battle, 17, 43–44, 47–48, 52
believer, 65, 69, 87
bloodline, 26–27

C

carnal, 41, 43
children, 26, 44, 47, 62
Christ, Jesus, 5, 32, 61, 70, 87

Christianity, 14, 87
church, 1, 4, 14, 25, 27, 32, 34, 46, 70, 80
comfort, 14–15, 38
complacency, 20
confusion, 3, 17, 20, 57
covenant, 16, 64
covet, 69, 90
curse, 27, 32, 40, 44

D

darkness, 4, 15, 28, 41, 47, 57
David, 47
Deborah, 46
deliverance, 3–4, 21–23, 25–30, 40, 83–84, 87
demons, 3–4, 25, 27, 29–30, 52, 61
destiny, 2, 5, 84
devil, 22, 29, 53, 85–86
direction, 64, 70
discernment, 41, 61, 63
dreams, 2–3, 5, 23, 25, 45, 64, 80, 84–85

E

Elijah, 79–80
Elisha, 79–80
enemy, 2, 15, 17, 22, 26, 28–30, 43–44, 46, 52–53, 57, 64, 75, 87
Evangelists, 53
eyes, 8, 12, 22, 24, 26, 38, 41, 50, 56, 58, 61, 82

F

faith, 30, 32–33, 69, 71, 74, 86
fear, 13, 35, 50, 61–62, 86
flesh, 20, 29, 33–35, 38–39, 45, 74, 85
flow, 25, 32, 69, 71, 74
fruit, 1, 3, 27, 57

G

gates, 65
gifts, 5, 8, 22, 31, 63, 69, 71, 74–75, 82, 85
   spiritual, 69, 71, 85
gospel, 29, 60–61, 78, 85
greatness, 38, 52

H

heaven, 2–3, 40, 61, 78, 81
holiness, 26, 31, 34, 74, 83
Holy Spirit, 29, 41, 46, 55, 57, 61–62, 64, 71, 73, 75, 79–80
honor, 38, 78
Hosea, 2, 15

I

intercession, 18, 53
Isaiah, 9, 70

J

Jehovah Jireh, 42
Jeremiah, 2–3, 41, 53, 74
Jezebel, 46
Joshua, 79–80
joy, 1, 7, 26, 34, 39, 44

K

kingdom, 34, 59, 83–84, 87
knowledge, 3, 15, 28, 67, 71, 84

L

law of God, 41, 78
leaders, 1, 4, 25, 84
leviathan, 46, 51, 84
Leviathan Spirit, 57
Lord's process, 37
love, 1, 14–15, 20, 23–24, 34, 40–42, 44, 47, 54, 59, 61–64, 68–71, 76, 82–84, 87

M

marriage, 16–17, 54, 63
ministry, 3–4, 29, 60, 70, 83
mouthpiece, 26, 74
Muslims, 10–11, 87

N

Nabiy, 72
nataph, 72, 90

O

Obscurity, 57
obstinacy, 39, 90
office, 2–3, 5, 55–56, 63, 77–78, 80

P

passion, 34
pastors, 4, 69–70, 82
Paul, 3
Pentecost, 75, 79
poems, 19, 28
position, 55, 77–78
praise, 38, 44, 70
pray, 2, 6, 10–11, 14, 46, 53, 56–57, 61–64, 82
prayer watches, 57, 78
Praying in tongues, 74–75
prophecy, 71, 77, 79
prophesy, 25, 56, 58, 65, 69, 71–73, 85–86
prophetic, 16, 25, 31, 67, 69, 71–74, 83
prophets, 1–3, 5, 19–20, 25, 41, 53, 55–56, 64, 70–71, 77–81
prophets love, 19–20
prophet's ministry, 1–2, 79
Psychics, 3

R

realms, 22, 54
rebellion, 23, 54, 70
rebuke, 34, 50
redemption, 17, 28
rejection, 14, 23
religion, 13, 19, 32, 34, 87
responsibility, 77
restoration, 18, 54
righteousness, 2, 26, 31, 33–34, 74

S

salvation, 7, 28, 47, 58
Samuel, 2
seer, 25
servant, 5, 8, 65, 68
Shamar, 2, 61–62
snares, 47, 53
soul, 4–5, 9, 16–18, 24, 29, 61
Sozo, 28
spiritual warfare, 22, 43–44, 46
strength, 23, 76
submission, 40
supernatural impartation, 69

T

teach, 2, 32, 36, 63, 68, 70, 83–87
Timothy, 36, 42, 62, 68
tongues, 24–25, 38, 61, 68, 71, 74–76
training, 56, 84, 86
truth, 5, 26, 28, 34, 47, 68

U

utterance, 32, 74

V

vagabond, 27, 90
visions, 2–3, 19, 38, 65, 73, 83
voice of God, 25, 27

W

water, 5, 37, 56, 64
wickedness, 2, 26
window, 12–13, 59, 61, 64
wisdom, 1, 3–4, 16, 68, 71
witchcraft, 3, 29, 33
worship, 35, 62, 68, 71–72

Z

Zechariah, 23

www.ingramcontent.com/pod-product-compliance
Lightning Source LLC
Chambersburg PA
CBHW071746080526
44588CB00013B/2162